Pieces of Longing

D1560362

ANONYMOUS

Pieces of Longing

Pieces of Longing Copyright © 2016 Anonymous.
All rights reserved. No part of this book may be used
or reproduced in any manner whatsoever without
written permission except in the case of reprints
in the context of reviews.

www.piecesoflonging.com

ISBN: 1537731564

ISBN-13: 978-1537731568

The further my journeys;
The sweeter my dreams.

CONTENTS

I

OASIS

Pieces of longing:
Your skin by the Bosphorus
Your breath in my ear

Tonight I am filled
With the sound of home
The hurry of the climbing moon
The rain flattening the reflections
On the harbour water

Tonight I am filled
With the apple
Of your tongue
The honey
Of your gasps
The secret knowledge
Of your clothes

Since I held you
The shape has gone out of steady things
The day lengthens like a moan
And the night is out of tune

When I leave you sleeping
You are as lost as one of my eyelashes
You rush into my thoughts
Like a gust of desert air
And your hair is full of
The scent of sand and stars

I chose my course
And can blame no one
That I set out upon it
I ran my seasons
Over the open mouths
Of so many waiting dunes

In my sky of wanting
I burned all I had
To stay aloft
Longing to find
A soft field that longed
For me to arrive

Now, like a lost pilot
I make my final turn
Toward the ground
There is no choice
Of landing place, no time
For the stars to realign

The planet rises
Under my hands
Like the body of a woman
I knew well
But never met

I have wanted
To follow your skin
Like falling water

Now I am almost
All dissolved
Shapeless
Quiet as a chrysalis

The world spins outside
And everything I thought I wanted
Begins to arrive on even tides
Thrown out of the sea
To litter my glittering beach

Wait

Wait for what will be me
To make sense of what I was
When I am unwrapped
Out of the dark silk sky

With the deep water lapping
At my naked feet
An empty empire
Full of new treasures

I still remember
The angle of the sun
Tearing though your dress
Beside the sugar cane fields

In the infinite surrender
I fell from the rim of your iris
Out of the limits of a body
Out of the cradle of the air

It was only the salt smell
Of broken waves in your hair
That caught me
That brought me back

Still, somewhere
I would like to hold you
The way the sun holds
A woman in love
Her face lit in a stray strand
Of the unruly morning
On her way down to the well
And there, I would like
To be unfolded the way
You open a letter in love
That is raw and new now
No matter how many times
You have already read those lines

It was as if
I fell backwards
Through your mouth
And the young smell of crushed grass
And the uncased movement of open time
And the sweet sleep of empty space

I only want a day
The same secret blue
Of an underwater shadow
A day that is as warm as you

A day made to repeat
Like a spoke in a spinning wheel
Until I am wound around you
Like a line returned to its reel

I only want a day
To make you love as long
As the sweeping summer
A day to write your song

I hold out in the hope that you
Will climb into the shape of my body
Even while the night is ebbing
Even when you are far away

Where is the woman
For one like me
Who is set to wandering
Like a moonless world

For one like me
Tied up in a single destiny
That keeps repeating
My ascendence and escape
Like an urgent word
Working through a drunken mind?

Where is the woman
For one like me
Who is set to sleeping
His life into one long dream
Of her extravagant laughter?

I go through the day now
Like the shadow of a bird
As hungry as a ghost
In an old set of clothes

When you ask
About the difference
Between the leaves
And the silk
The colour of mulberries
Spreads over your clothes
Your skin
Your mouth

The shadows of leaves
Play on you like watered silk
Soft as wild honey

Show me again and I'll believe
The best things I've seen
Have been forgotten

Oh now, for a simple dawn
That only asks the time
And rolls away laughing

In a single room
With one wide window
Open to the newness of the day

Was it cruel
To adorn your summer body
With those silver chains
And then strike out through the ocean
In my elemental hope?

How definite was
The idea of you
That it could stand to be thought
So many times
Without breaking?

I know you knew
If any of it could

Have been true
Even once
It would have been you

Life is short
But because
I want you
The afternoon
Is so long

I bring these
Paper flowers
For you to eat
These scraps of me
To litter your doorway
These pieces of longing
For you to discard

Sofia
how did I
already know
your name
Sofia?

The wandering sky is closed
A grey veil is drawn over
Your many stars

The moment is completely gone
The apple of your skin
Is hidden again

You may even have forgotten
The dark, sacred shapes
My hands could make

But I can still taste the time
It took the moon to climb
Your shoulder-blades

The sun has slipped
Down the lemon trees
And the unraveled day turns
The colour of your hair

The sky lightens
On the landscape of your body
Your robe ripples like a field of wheat
Under the wind of my hands

The way you have untied your hair
Has untied all my plans
And left my resolve resting
Against a corner of your cheek

When you look for me in the winter
I will be full of warm remembering
And summer thoughts of your eyes
Will always find the way to my cold skin

Come, sit
Tonight your hands
Have held the coldest flowers
And their dew beads on us
Like pearls of air

I have known you
In a familiar garden
In a dream of the sun
Running through your hair
Like thoughts of home
Like my stranger's hands

The earth is warm and moves
Alive and lit by light
From another day
I am watching some future fruit form
And your body is made of it
Shall I say the word
Or are you sick with it?
Shall I say the word
Or will we save it?

Give me horizon
A mouthful of wine
Your mouth as open
As a broken fig
And then the far
Far deep water

When you ask me
Why I want you
I want to rise up
On one elbow
And explain
The shape of honey
The taste of your name
The colour of the sea

You come to me
Out of those deep sheets
Your small breasts soft
In the clutch of midnight
Your quiet gasps close
In the press of summer

Find me a picture of a place
Where it's not raining
Bring me a mirror with a face
That isn't straining
To see into tomorrow
Or asking to borrow my skin

Now take off your dress
And show me the shape
Of the golden thing
We're about to make

That we'll worship throughout
Our other hours
Until the bells are ringing
In all the towers
And we've sold all your earrings
And can't afford flowers
And we run out of wine
And coffee, and time

Green river
So quiet
At your simple task
Of bearing love
To all your branches
Here I'm woven
Within your water
The tired dream
Of your silk shoulders
And heavy fruit
Full, under a vast, unfurling future
Of sky and silt
Make me one more island
Overrun by hyacinth
Make me one more child
In your tree of worlds

Mekong Delta, Vietnam 2016

Another day
In my paper world
As a salesman
Who was himself sold
Into a journey
For further dreams
And a deeper need

It gets under my fingernails
Gets into my marrow
And makes me weather
These slings and arrows
As necessary as bee stings
On the path to honey
As necessary as breath is
To a string of pearls

So am I strung like veins
In an eye tired by staring
At the borrowed dark
For a hint of tomorrow

I see you on the terrace
Reaching for purple figs
Your hair in your eyes
The sun tearing
Through your dress
You cannot know
How I watch you

After a dream
Has been burned up
Like bright red unfolding
Flowers, full of the air
Of madness

After a dream
Has left me longing
Wandering the wild
Untouched reaches
Of my need for you

After a dream
Has left my dull body
Lying alone in a hotel bed
I fade into a memory
Of someone else I used to be

II

ISLAND

I listen for your heartbeat
Somewhere through a wall
Through a black wave of time
From deep within you
Through the fabric
Of the sea
I think I can hear it
Thudding like footsteps
On a cold beach at low tide
The bones of these islands
Are set to trembling
It is carried to me
Through the limbs of the earth
When I lie on the hill
I think I can hear it
Through my jaw
Your living drum
In my temple
Calling me to worship
Calling me home
A lost vessel
In the iron mouth
Of the ocean
Hearing the faint
Plea to return
I realise now

I may have been
Returning to you
All my life

When you lie in the sea
Your limbs become
A thousand flying fishes
That leap like opalescent kites
When I reach for them
You disappear

When you lie in the sea
And your eyes close in the sun
I am washed away
And seagulls carry me
On their plaintive cries
Across the world

When you lie in the sea
Your skin becomes a day
Pregnant with the music
Of palm fronds
As full as the spring tide
Of your beauty

Under the water
You are wild; your naked legs
Taunt the jealous sea

When the sea is round
As a new peach
Or when she's haggard
And harrows the beach
With silver claws
Still I love you
With a full tide of love

You gather me up
Like a collection of shells
Someone cast away

I am caught
In the current of her name
A riptide that quietly decides
To tear the ocean open
And drop my heart
Behind the furthest wave
Like a falling moon
That no one sees
And no one saves

When I lie down with you
In my threadbare clothes
You open to me
Like the sea drawing back
To show its dark bones
Its treasured shells
Its purest sand

Reach for me
With your nightly
Insomniac phone calls
With your little noises of assent
With your blue fingernails
Like careful birds
Landing on my sleeping chest
Reach for me when I'm raw and rippling
Under the strength of my paper dreams
Under the weight of the tropical dark
Breathing the water out of the air
In gasps that are drawn like the black waves
Tonguing the beach outside

The night is bound around your hips
And holds you low and tight
Your dream is as cold as your lips
Washed in neon light

America is on tonight
America is bright
You see the thing she made you be
It's real but not quite right

We're coming down; we've run aground
The end of one more flight
And home is just a place we found
To keep us out of sight

All I own is future
All I want is sky

Now my colour dissolves
With yours in oil and sea
We're free to bleed across
The canvas of this country
And so with no way to go slow
We take up our paper clothes
And our quickened hearts and run
For all the borders at once

Now I am here
Where they are not burning the day
And you are not waking up
Like honey sliding off a spoon
And your body
Has not become wine

Raffles Hotel, Singapore 2016

The dream is a cocktail at Sloppy Joe's –
The bloom blown so far off the Havana rose
The rows and rows of crumbling shadows
Maybe it is, but nobody knows.

The dream wore blue on the airport road –
Her gold hair high and her laugh echoes
Through miles and miles of open windows
Maybe it's her, but nobody knows.

Sloppy Joe's, Havana 2016

Havana
Her heat has
Peeled this city open
And the night can arrive
On a bright gun-carriage
With its little revolutions
Blue and yellow and spinning
Each as glorious as a match flame
And some bronze drunkard
Sits, smirking in the corner
Because the waiters
Will never fill
The empty
Tourists

La Bodegita Del Medio, Havana 2016

Stories have no end;
Countries have no lines.
Everything you think you know
May be blurred and remade
In other lights, at other times,
By steady notes on a simple guitar,
Or by the white, lunar seas
Reflected on the necks
Of soft-edged women.

Hello again great lady, Time
Who knows too much
About what is mine
And what is just

Outside the reach
Of my perfect rage
On the bones of a beach
In an ivory cage

In the atrocities of
The flashing lights
Goodbye my friend
Who could buy the night

I enter the heart
On narrow gauge
Through the growling dark
My thirst assuaged

I come upon
A thing to do
A man to be
Someone new

Raffles Hotel, Singapore 2016

Although I know
I must kiss you now
I do not
Every kiss is a promise
When I think of the promises
I have yet to keep
I do not kiss you

Darling, stay
Why must you always run away?
By now I've learned enough
To know for those like us
Home is a place
We'll always chase

Here I am
Caught in a jar of silence
Brittle as a cold drop of glass
As slight as the slight leaves in the afternoon
The sun going through me
Through the palm trees
Through the surface of the sea
Long is the road to restitution
The reclamation of a tin crown
That fell by a deep bed
Where my heart was sleeping
When I was far away
And had forgotten all the pearls
At the bottom of the bay
That I was told were mine
And, waking now
To the swifter current of the years
To a sweet need to be redeemed
By the furthest reaches of my arms
I have remembered all my dreams

I have lived so long
In the prophecy of myself
I forgot the shape of a woman
Is like a perfect shell
As open to today
As the coast is open
To the ocean

Writing is
Going down
To the opal sea
To keep me from drying out
Like a mouth soaked in whisky
I will come back
Clean as the bones of trees

Bring me your mouth
And your mystery

Now, cast away
Your wings and your shells
And stand there proud and quivering
A white, unsheeted sail
Your lines all undone
By my hands

Let sleep find me here
Deep in our last afternoon
In your Spanish hair

Wild hearts
Don't break;
They burn
Blue as
Driftwood
Their salt flames
As hungry as the
Midnight mouths
Of empty hearths
As long and open
As a castaway
Madness

Greenwich Hotel, New York 2016

Ten thousand of these
Anonymous dreams
I've had and spilled and still
You'll find me awake
On a mattress
Flat on the floor
Of my tin shack

Come back if you want
But come quietly
To hear me untie
All your histories
And perhaps one night
To hand you over
To your lost mystery
One more time

Stay with me
While the turning stars
Go through the palm leaves
While we both still feel
The pull of the sea's need
While there's still fruit to feed on
While you still read these
Anonymous dreams

When my knees give in
And I am old
Encase me in a suit
Wheel me to the sea
And sometimes
Come to kiss my head
With all the sweetness
Of pity

I should have written
My poems about your skin
Onto your skin
Along your ribs
Where the questions
Between men
And women
Begin

Jewel of the sea
Gold of the east
I cannot claim to know anything
But the shores you lead me to
Why can you not always
Be this way with me?
When you are wilful and difficult
And drag me to the rocks
To drown me
How do I love you
In your rages?
Barefoot and beggared
In your bones
Bailing out the water of hope
From both our bodies
We can go on a little longer, love
There are still secret places in you
My devotion will discover
The splinters in your heart
That my ready hands will smooth away
And so, still, at the end of the day
We'll turn together
For the low red sun
And plunge through the wake
And reach home as one

Alessandra
I could watch your hands
Cut strawberries
All morning

III

DESERT

My grandfather
Rode tanks
Grew dahlias

Crossed deserts
Dug trenches

And soaked the earth
With water
From a broken flower pot

If you will not
Give yourself to me
I will climb out of this bed
Out of my own reflection
Through the desert dust
And the purple stones
With the few things I still carry
And my lungs clean
But my heart will rust

My love always opens
In your jasmine lap
Like the favourite part
Of a cherished book

Since I met you
My crooked spine
And dog-eared pages
All point to you

Today, we can fall together
With the ease
Of late afternoon shadows
Against a wall

Because
I want you
My afternoon is clear
The sky is clear
The rest
Of my life
Is clear

There are no new names
For the slow savagery of the dunes
For the night on the desert
For the silk folds in the lap of time
That will cover everything

But when you lie with me
I want new words to blossom
Over your body like a secret meadow
On a high, hidden plateau
That can only be reached by air

The longer I don't know you
The wilder I become.

The softer my memory;
The harder my hands.

The further my journeys;
The sweeter my dreams.

I am bound by the things
My fingers can make
In a world as misshapen
As a freshwater pearl

When the wind howls
Through the sunlight
I am brought a broken breath
Of a perfume I've always sought

Sometimes I think when the day is dark
Your eyes must be as soft
As the highest piece of sky
That reaches a hidden reef

Where are you hiding now
That the air is so rife with clues of you?
Are you already here, somewhere in
The longest days of my life?

When you come along
I'll dismantle my watch
And set time free on the sand
Like a scuttling crab

When you come along
I'll take up a sarong and a paintbox
And cover the world
With new canvas
And fresh sailcloth
And there will be new things to say
On the streets I've known too well
At every point along the way
Where I've had to hustle and sell

When you come along
My voice will change
My eyes will soften
And it will be an era
Of blue forgetting and bright remembering
I will forget the reasons for building
These shining towers
And I will remember
The seasons I have dreamed
I will forget faces
The words of songs

And remember wisps of tunes
I'll whistle in endless loops
On long ferry rides
In foreign supermarkets
So that you will always find me
On the far edge of the world

On nights like these
The body turns
Words like leaves
Are shaken from you
And August also rains

I awake
From a green haze
Days later
At the middle of the maze
With no answers

Somewhere
A train passes
And I think the tremor
In my heart
Might have been set
By your white fingers

Like a poisoned seed
That is watered
By disappointments
By missed connections
By delayed flights
By long lengths of waiting

When I see you naked
I cannot tell
If you are a wing
Or a shell

I begin to understand
You must be one of
The daughters
Of the world

Look at me:
Just a man
Who must have
Fallen out of the dust

Your name is still
Curling in my mouth
Like cigar smoke

Because
I asked it of you
You gave me the ends
Of all your ribbons
To tie or untie
As I liked

Because
I asked it of you
You gave me your riddled day
To test the answers of my heart

Because
I have lain
So long alone
Beside you

Because
I must find
The way through the door
That only you saw

Because
The world is whirling on its edge
And I am whirling in the colour
Of your dancing

High and wild
And spinning

Because
When I look up
From my mine of madness
I am a child in the sand again
And the sea has been roaring
Outside my tiny walls
All along

Because
The fear
Of not being heard
Must be greater
Than the fear
Of standing up

Because
I've learnt to live on
Horizon
And the shy smiles of women
And the sweet taste
Of water on skin

I have become this thing
A voice with half a face
A throat that will not sing
A picture out of place

The moment I am known
Is the moment I must leave
I have become this thing
That cannot bear to grieve

A reason to regret
A story on a shelf
A promise to forget
I never made myself

I bent down to my work
I bent down to your kiss
If I was said to kneel
It was only for your bliss

Sweet pearl
Bitter moon
The rising tide
Will meet us soon
And my tired back
My leaking roof
Will be carried as
The burden of proof
That I now am
A better man
Good woman, come
Make better use
Of your sure hands
Unknit my brow
Take off this yoke
That chokes me now

We will go in like guerrillas
Low and secret in the dark
We will go in behind the wet leaves
And under the rail bridges
And under the cover of grey rain
We will go in with our hearts
Warmed by the match-flame of hope
Flickering between our fingers
Boots worn, a few ragged clothes
That won't dry on a sagging line
A few ragged lines we keep repeating
To anyone who'll listen
To keep us going in
For the new fight that is beginning
On some Saturdays we will feel the sun
Breaking over the cold
And our faces will turn for the upcountry
We will go in and shelter
In the overlooked places
In workshops and whorehouses
And rest the barrels of our dreams
Against the peeling leaded walls
Of midnight cafés
And keep scratching at the problem
Until it festers and a healing fever blooms
There is no marching

But there is movement
There is no motion
But there is change

My love is
On the ground
Scattered
Like ripe apples
On an orchard floor
If you look closely
You can still
Find firm flesh
A faithful heart
Perfect fruit

Love
Where are you that I cannot find you?
I have dragged myself here
To know
How far I have to go
The east is still heavy
With promises
As clear as liquid glass
In the scalding shapes of tears
I see now how much
I have to do
To reach that far shore
But how must it be done
Without you?

You come to me again
As if the year had not begun
As if my skin had unlearned
How to yearn for yours
As if your heart was not already sold
As if someone in a crowd had told us
The world was about to happen
As it happened that day
Laid out as surely as an apple
On a picnic blanket
Where the grass was tall
And wet with morning

My dreams
Have gone
Through me
Like flocks of birds
They leave me behind
My face creased by the bed
And twelve hours of exhausted sleep

Last night I looked for you
And you were everywhere
In the corners of my vision
In the ticket stubs
Of my journeys
In the pages
Of memory
I tore out

As I sat on my suitcase
Waiting for a plane
To take me closer to you
Or send me, insane
Across the world, raving

Racing like a pulse
That knew your touch
And then felt it

On the new skin
Of a new wrist
On the first day
Of a new life

And time, wheeling
Over my little words and works
Strikes me again and again
With the angle of its angry hands
With its coy looks
With its wry smiles
With its unfolded map
Of miles and miles of empty sand

So I search
In the far dunes
In the long seams
Of further and further dreams
For the clues to the other half
In shards of shattered glass

Tokyo blue
The morning feeds you
With many flavoured roses
With warm hands full
Of patient strawberries
The sickle moon
Swings through the wheat
It sets in the high arches
Of her freed feet
In the heart of the river
It falls in its halves,
Naked and red
In the red of her hair
In the red of the street

Once again
I am unfolded
Like an old page
You keep
But cannot
Bear to read

The moon is on the right
The moon is on the right
The highest Tokyo light
Like a half orange, bitten open.

The contract is written
That these days will lead other days
And nothing can change
Or be woken
And love may wax and wane
By ancient stages
By slow earthquakes
That wake the body
And still the soul's alarm.

How soon will the night
Be made whole
In the loophole
Of your arms?

Imperial Palace Gardens, Tokyo

Now I am
Particularly sleepless
The Chateau is muted
And heavy with goodbyes
At one in the morning
Sunday is gone
You are gone
Even the perfect sound
Of your departing shoes
Is gone

Chateau Marmont, Hollywood

The sun goes down
With the bell and the howl
Six o'clock in the old town
Panama begins to prowl
And serve her rum spiced
And drink with one swallow
And say dangerous things like
Creo que te amo

Panama City

Take all my love
All the leaves I've left
As gifts for wayward doves
The olives for their theft
The peace after the flood
The desert page bereft
Of ink and wine and blood
A heart dispossessed
Of beauty in its bud
A soul that cannot rest
And take all my love

Here is the movement
Of a spirit that must move
The wild-haired wandering
Of a sunburned madness
The eremitic journey
Of my ceaseless hope

Here is the love
Of a heart that must
Have heard of love once
And now rasps against
The smoothest days
Like a stubbled cheek
Against a silk thigh

Here is the work
Of hands that must work
And can only rest in the blue shade
Of your quiet breasts
Like two labourers asleep
In the heat of the day
Deep in a gold wheat field
Under perfect hills of hay

In the dream you were a dancer
Caught up in the loose liquid chord
The champagne twilight was swaying
With the gifts I still could afford

And the night filled with gold and illusion
The blue cello felt through your limbs
Oh my love, dream again
My star is high; your tide is in

You moved in the shape of a body
Along a song that cannot be sung
In a room filled with crystalline lotus
Where the old come to bask in the young

And the light may know all of your secrets
And your heart may still beat out a hymn
Oh my love, dream again
My star is high; your tide is in

You caved to the reason of dreamers
For a season of perpetual thrall
You dropped all the leaves of your clothing
That were called to the floor by the fall

And a million eyes wrestled for you
And the rise of the blush on your skin
Oh my love, dream again
My star is high; your tide is in

Now the keys of your heart will be copied
The pins will align in the lock
Could the red of your mouth still be spinning
Behind a door that I didn't knock

When the vision has yet to be painted
And the day has to ask to begin
Oh my love, dream again
My star is high; your tide is in

In the palm of a morning I left you
To bloom like a flame on the sky
The shadows stream past on the highway
The way most of my life has gone by

And where in the sea am I sent to
And where in the night have you been
Oh my love, dream again
My star is high; your tide is in

At last
You see it
The path is lit
The stars hold fast
At last the dark
Lets out the tide
The sea retreats
The roar subsides
The outcast wins
You outswim the past
At last
At last

CPSIA information can be obtained
at www.ICGtesting.com
Printed in the USA
BVOW08s1925211216
471542BV00002B/134/P

9 781537 731568